WILD HORSES

A SPIRIT UNBROKEN

Text copyright © 1995 by Elwyn Hartley Edwards

Printed in China

First hardcover edition
95   96   97   98   99   5   4   3   2   1
First softcover edition
04   5   4

Library of Congress Cataloging-in-Publication Data available
ISBN 0-89658-271-X (hardcover)   ISBN 0-89658-516-6 (softcover)

Distributed in Canada by Raincoast Books, 9050 Shaughnessy Street, Vancouver, B.C. V6P 6E5
Published by Voyageur Press, Inc. 123 North Second Street, P.O. Box 338, Stillwater, MN 55082 U.S.A.
651-430-2210, fax 651-430-2211   books@voyageurpress.com   www.voyageurpress.com

Educators, fundraisers, premium and gift buyers, publicists, and marketing managers:
Looking for creative products and new sales ideas? Voyageur Press books are available at special
discounts when purchased in quantities, and special editions can be created to your specifications.
For details contact the marketing department at 800-888-9653.

Photographs © 1995 by:

Front cover © Gary Leppart
Back cover © Charles G. Summers JR
Page 1 © Charles G. Summers JR
Page 4 © Gary Leppart
Page 6 © Gary Leppart
Page 9 © Only Horses Picture Agency
Page 10 © Rita Summers
Page 11 © Gary Leppart
Page 12 © Charles G. Summers JR
Page 13 © Gary Leppart
Page 14 © Charles G. Summers JR
Page 15 © Gary Leppart
Page 16 © Gary Leppart
Page 19 © Only Horses Picture Agency
Page 21 © Gary Leppart
Page 22 © Sally Anne Thompson (Animal
Photography)
Page 23 © Bob Langrish
Page 24 © Bob Langrish
Page 27 © Bob Langrish
Page 28 © Sally Anne Thompson (Animal
Photography)
Page 31 © David Currey (NHPA)
Page 32 © Michael Leach (NHPA)
Page 35 © R. Willbie (Animal Photography)
Page 36 © Sally Anne Thompson (Animal
Photography)
Page 39 TOP © Only Horses Picture Agency
Page 39 BOTTOM © Only Horses Picture
Agency

Page 40 © Sally Anne Thompson (Animal
Photography)
Page 41 TOP © R. Willbie (Animal Photography)
Page 41 BOTTOM © Bob Langrish
Page 42 © Henry Ausloos (NHPA)
Page 45 TOP © Only Horses Picture Agency
Page 45 BOTTOM © Only Horses Picture
Agency
Page 46 © Only Horses Picture Agency
Page 47 © Christer Fredriksson (Bruce Coleman)
Page 48 © Bob Langrish
Page 49 TOP © Bob Langrish
Page 49 BOTTOM © Bob Langrish
Page 50 © Henry Ausloos (NHPA)
Page 51 © Only Horses Picture Agency
Page 52 © Bob Langrish
Page 55 © Bob Langrish
Page 56 © Bob Langrish
Page 59 © Pat and Rosemary Keough
Page 60 © Pat and Rosemary Keough
Page 63 © Bob Langrish
Page 64 © Pat and Rosemary Keough
Page 65 © Pat and Rosemary Keough
Page 66 © Sally Anne Thompson (Animal
Photography)
Page 67 © Sally Anne Thompson (Animal
Photography)
Page 68 © Gary Leppart
Page 71 © Gary Leppart
Page 72 © Charles G. Summers JR

Page 74 © Bob Langrish
Page 75 © Otto Rogge (ANT-NHPA)
Page 76 © Charles G. Summers JR
Page 77 © Gary Leppart
Page 78 © Charles G. Summers JR
Page 79 © Charles G. Summers JR
Page 80 © Gary Leppart
Page 81 © Gary Leppart
Page 82 © Anthony Bannister (NHPA)
Page 83 © Otto Rogge (NHPA)
Page 84 © Gary Leppart
Page 85 © Gary Leppart
Page 86 © Charles G. Summers JR
Page 87 © Gary Leppart
Page 88 © Steve Robinson (NHPA)
Page 91 © E. Hanumantha Rao (NHPA)
Page 92 © E. A. Janes (NHPA)
Page 94 © Nigel J. Dennis (NHPA)
Page 95 © Nigel J. Dennis (NHPA)
Page 96 © Gary Leppart
Page 98 © Gary Leppart
Page 99 © Rita Summers
Page 100 © Rita Summers
Page 103 © Bob Langrish
Page 104 © David E. Rowley (Planet Earth)
Page 105 © Gary Leppart
Page 106 © Gary Leppart
Page 107 © Gary Leppart
Page 108 © Charles G. Summers JR
Page 109 © Gary Leppart

WILD HORSES

A Spirit Unbroken

Elwyn Hartley Edwards

Voyageur Press

CONTENTS

HORSES IN THE WILD

The 'true' horse, scientifically named *Equus caballus*, evolved a million years ago as the culmination of an evolutionary process extending over 60 millennia. The early ancestors of the horse were small, multi-toed creatures, about the size of a fox and in no way resembling the horses of today. In accordance with the inexorable laws of survival, they had to adapt to the slowly changing environment like all developing species. By the Pleistocene period, some six million years ago when secondary forest-type vegetation had given way to a savannah environment supporting wiry grasses, an animal recognisable as a horse was becoming established on the North American continent. This was *Pliohippus*, and was distinguished by being the first animal in the progression leading to *Equus* that had a single hoof. *Pliohippus* represents the lead-in to *Equus* proper and also for the sub-generic group of zebras, asses and 'hemionids', the 'half-asses'.

Five million years after the prototype *Pliohippus*, *Equus caballus*, in possibly as many as 20 forms, as well as its related Equidae, had spread from North America over the connecting landbridges into Asia, South America, Europe and Africa.

Towards the end of the Ice Age, in perhaps 9,000 BC, the receding ice sheets carried away those landbridges and the American continent with its horse population was effectively isolated. At some point, probably 8,000 years or more ago, the horse became extinct in the Americas for reasons which have never been established. It was not until the arrival of the Spanish *conquistadores* in the sixteenth century, bringing horses with them for the conquest of Mexico, that the species was re-introduced to the continent in which to all intents it originated.

Equus, however, continued its development in the Old World, finally emerging in three principal forms of horse in Europe and Western Asia. Herds of asses and zebras inhabited the north and south of Africa, respectively, and large numbers of onager were to be found in the Middle East.

For a million years or so the horse herds were a more or less convenient larder on the hoof for the swiftly evolving human race and the cave-art of Cro-Magnon man, executed 15-20,000 years ago at Lascaux in France and Santander in Spain, for instance, provides vivid evidence of the relationship.

Domestication of the horse came later, 5-6,000 years ago, at the end of the Neolithic period. It seems almost certain that it first took place in Eurasia, through the agency of nomadic Aryan tribes, and was probably centred in the steppes

7

around the Black and Caspian Seas. The horse-people of the Eurasian steppe-lands kept their herds in a semi-feral state, as, indeed, they do to this day, but it is from this point in the history of the world that the existence of truly wild horses begins to decline, their place being taken by domestic stock.

Of the three principal forms of horse, the 'founding fathers' of the post-glacial period which are discussed in the following chapter, the Asiatic Horse of pre-history is still preserved in zoological parks throughout the world, although very recently a group has been returned to the wild. However, the second of the three, the original Tarpan of Eastern Europe and the Ukranian steppes had been hunted to extinction by the late eighteenth century. Nonetheless, what may be termed a 're-constituted' Tarpan, closely resembling the original, has been created by breeding back to surviving mixed stock and is kept in semi-feral herds in the forest reserves of Popielno and Bialowieza in Poland.

Of the last of the trio, the heavy Forest or Diluvial horse, there is no trace, except in the presence of its far-removed descendants, the various heavy horse breeds of Europe. Other than the horse-herds of the Asian steppes, pockets of horses and ponies, still living to all intents in the natural state, have survived into the twentieth century, despite the pressures of a shrinking environment. The last truly wild horses are the Mustangs of America, now increasingly protected, and the still numerous Brumbies of the Australian outback.

With occasional exceptions, the zebra family was never domesticated and large wild herds still exist in Southern Africa, although only three species now survive. By 1878, for example, the last of the wild quaggas had disappeared from the plains south of the Vaal river, having been exterminated by Boer farmers who shot them to feed their workers. The last quagga in captivity died in the Amsterdam Zoo in 1883. Less numerous than the zebras is the sub-genus *Hemionus* inhabiting Western Asia, India and the Middle East.

The Persian Onager (*Equus hemionus onager*) is probably extinct in the wild, but the Indian Onager, or Ghorkar (*Equus hemionus khur*) probably continues to exist in small numbers in the Indian Desert. In fact, there are still Mongolian Kulans (*Equus hemionus hemionus*) in the desert areas of Central Asia and some Kiang herds (*Equus hemionus kiang*) on the high steppes of the Tibetan plateau.

'The white horses of the sea' in their salt-laden homeland of
France's Camargue region. The horses of the Camargue, living in herds
(manades) as they have done from time immemorial, are of ancient origin
and were probably indigenous to the area in prehistoric times.

9

Dawn in Wyoming, a state rich in Mustang history, where
enthusiasts have sought to restore and perpetuate the old Spanish strains
of 400 years ago from which the Mustangs are descended.

*Wyoming Mustang stallion on the summer range. The
common Mustang coat colour ranges through all shades of dun,
but Pinto colouring, originating with the early Spanish imports,
is also found in Mustang herds.*

Although much reduced in number, the Mustang
population is now preserved in supervised wild horse refuges and is
protected by law against the depredations of hunters.

The tough, hardy Mustang stock is well able to survive

the rigours of the weather. There are also a number of societies which

work to ensure the welfare of the wild herds by preserving the natural

habitat, maintaining the supply of water and providing

essential minerals like salt.

THE WILD FOUNDATION

The last of the founding fathers of the equine races is the Asiatic Wild Horse (Equus caballus przewalskii przewalskii). Nicholai Przewalskii, the Russian explorer, discovered wild herds in the Tachin Schah Mountains in 1879.

The surviving link between the modern horse and those of pre-history is provided by the Asiatic Wild Horse. In simplistic terms this horse (*Equus przewalskii przewalskii poliakov*) and its contemporary, the lighter-built Tarpan (*Equus caballus gmelini antonius*), are seen as the ancestors of the world's light horse breeds. The development of the heavy horse breeds is attributed to the Forest Horse (*Equus caballus silvaticus*), the slow-moving, browsing animal of the forested swamplands of post-glacial northern Europe.

In fact, since development can never be a matter of precise boundaries, there has to have been an element of cross-fertilisation between all three of the 'primitive' wild horses and then, importantly and continuously, between the cross-bred derivatives which formed the herds of the early, nomadic horse-peoples.

For thousands of years following the recession of the ice packs, the habitat of the Asiatic Wild Horse extended all over the European and Central Asian steppes, merging into the territory of the lighter Tarpan along the line drawn by longitude 40. However, the 'primitive' wild horses were never a subject for domestication and as the steppe stock became increasingly diluted by cross-breeding, the numbers of the truly wild ancestors decreased commensurately, surviving only in the least accessible areas; in the instance of the Asiatic Wild Horse, in the mountains flanking the Gobi Desert in Mongolia, where climatic conditions are as severe as any in the world.

The existence of wild horse herds was known to the Kirghiz people, who were to hunt the animals to the point of extinction, but it was not until the nineteenth century that Europe was made aware of their presence and began to appreciate their unique significance.

In 1814 the English naturalist and explorer Col. Hamilton Smith obtained detailed descriptions of herds moving around the edges of the Gobi Desert and published his findings in Vol. 20 of *Jardine's Naturalists Library*. However, the discovery in 1879 by the explorer Nicolai Mikhailovitch Przewalskii, of wild herds in the Tachin Schah Mountains (literally, the 'Mountains of the Yellow Horse') bordering the Gobi, provided the real springboard for scientific study of this influential early form of *Equus caballus*.

Przewalskii, a Colonel in the Imperial Russian army, was neither a zoologist nor a naturalist. He was, in fact, an agent for his government, who, along with their British counterparts, sought to influence the power structure among the tribes of

Central Asia abutting the northern parts of British India. Both were involved in the map-making and surveying that would be necessary if military operations were ever to be undertaken. Although highly regarded in his field as a tenacious traveller of determination and insatiable curiosity, it was as the discoverer of the earliest form of *Equus* that Przewalskii was to achieve immortality.

It was on a Wild Horse skin obtained by Przewalskii that the zoologist J S Poliakov based his first scientific studies, cataloguing the sub-species in 1881. Within 10 years of Przewalskii's discovery Russian and European collectors and zoologists, with the aid of Kirghiz hunters, had obtained sufficient live specimens to form a breeding nucleus which was subsequently responsible for the captive stock of the present day.

The Asiatic Wild Horse differs uniquely from modern stock, not least because of a chromosome count of 66 rather than the usual 64. In appearance it is just as distinctive. The coat colour is a sandy dun with the underbelly a deep cream. The legs, mane and tail are black, and the former can be horizontally striped like those of a zebra. Usually, there is a pronounced dorsal stripe of dark hair, often accompanied by a similarly coloured cross over the shoulder. The colouring is a reminder of the protective coat pattern of the early equine ancestors. As a form of camouflage their coats are considered to have been blotched or striped. The mane grows upright and the hair texture, like that on the lower half of the tail, is harsh. Unusually, the Wild Horse has no forelock – the head, too, is noticeably different in detail. It is heavy with a long, convex profile and the eyes are set high and close to the ears. The animal measures about 13h.h (132cm) at the wither and is straight-backed, like zebras and asses, reflecting clearly the close proximity of a common, prehistoric root.

Even in captivity Przewalskii's Horse can never be considered as tame and no-one has ever attempted to school one to saddle or harness, a feat occasionally accomplished with the zebra and much more frequently with the onager, which preceded the horse as the motive power of the pre-Christian chariot. Both stallions and mares are unusually fierce and aggressive, far more so than domestic stock and will act in concert to counter any attack by predators. There is also a special 'primitive vigour' in the wild horses manifested in the feral state by very high fertility levels and exceptional qualities of constitution, stamina and spirit.

Whilst in some respects Przewalskii's Horse tends towards the asinine characteristics, the Tarpan, 'is a type more specialised towards the horse' (W Salensky 1907).

The 'modern' Tarpan, re-constituted by selective breeding from descendant strains, is preserved in the Popielno and Bialowieza herds.

The Tarpan (literally 'wild horse') ranged widely over eastern Europe and the Ukranian steppes but in its original form it certainly did not survive in any numbers into the latter part of the eighteenth century, for it was intensively hunted and even at that point the true wild animals had mated with domestic stock. It was first observed scientifically by the Russian-German scientist J F Gmelin, who captured four wild specimens in Russia in 1768. It was subsequently catalogued in the 1920s by Helmut Otto Antonius, the one time Director of the Schonbrunn Zoological Gardens in Vienna and an acknowledged authority on the sub-species.

The Tarpan was about the same height as Przewalskii's Horse but much lighter in build with long, slender legs. It was more refined than its contemporary, particularly in the head, although the profile remained convex to a degree. Otherwise, it had the expected characteristics of an animal evolving in dry, steppe-type conditions, and like the onagers, living in similar conditions, it was swift in movement.

Antonius considered the Tarpan influence to have extended from the Carpathians through to Turkestan and beyond. The Hucal and Konik ponies of the Ukraine are certainly descendants of the Tarpan and it was to these the Polish authorities returned when they attempted to re-constitute the Tarpan in the Popielno and Bialowieza herds. They selected those animals which on the evidence available had retained the most pronounced Tarpan character, and with great skill bred back to selected strains. The result has to be accepted as a fairly accurate replica of the original wild horse which, even more remarkably, has retained much of the primitive qualities that are not found in so great a degree in later domestic stock.

The colour of the horses and the peculiar coat texture corresponds with the descriptions given by Gmelin. The coat hair is wiry in texture, like that of a deer, with the colour varying between mouse- and blue-dun. The dorsal stripe, like that of the Przewalskii, is prominent and is usually accompanied by barred, zebra markings on the legs and sometimes by similar stripes on the body. The coat, like that of many truly wild creatures, turns white in severe winter conditions.

Surprisingly, the 'new' Tarpan remains an example of the unique 'primitive vigour' that accounts for its dominant influence on subsequent domestic stock. It is exceptionally hardy and independent to the point of being fierce. It has a strength quite disproportionate to its size, exceptional powers of endurance and stamina and quite remarkable strength of constitution. Abortion is unknown in the herds and the fertility rate is very high. The animals rarely suffer sickness and it has been observed that even deep wounds heal with unusual speed and never require outside attention, if, indeed, the animal would allow itself to be handled.

Although mainland Europe has numerous pony breeds and types deriving from the early, post-glacial stock, Germany has only one – the Dülmen. It fulfils no practical purpose, and is of interest because it is kept privately in semi-feral conditions on the estate of the Dukes of Croy in the Meerfelder Bruch, Westphalia, where it is said the ponies have been bred since the early fourteenth century. The ponies are in consequence, of mixed blood, crosses have frequently been made to Polish stock having a predominant Tarpan background, as well as to British pony stallions. The Dülmen herd resembles the British New Forest breed in some respects, but exhibits less fixity of type and colouring. The ponies are usually just under 13h.h (132cm) and have a reputation for being sound and very hardy.

PRZEWALSKII'S HORSE

The sole German pony breed is the Dülmen. It can be
seen on the estates of the Dukes of Croy in Westphalia where it is
claimed that the ponies have been bred since the fourteenth century.
The modern ponies are of diverse origin. This study of the Asiatic
Wild Horse (opposite), reveals much of its primitive character.

THE UNIVERSAL PROVIDER

This is the American version of the Bashkir pony, whose homeland is Bashkiria in the Ural foothills.

The North American continent has to be accepted as the cradle of the equine race, but the development of the species after the Ice Age belongs indubitably to the vast Eurasian steppelands which have supported huge horse herds for thousands of years. Because of them, the nomadic tribes embraced a horse culture upon which their existence depended, and even today the economy of the steppe people remains surprisingly reliant upon horse herds kept in much the same semi-feral conditions that have pertained since the beginning of recorded time.

Outer Mongolia still has the largest number of horses per head of population in the world, and despite the inevitable incursions of modernity, horses continue to be central to the people's lifestyle. They provide meat, dairy products and the much valued *kummis*, a fermentation that is the fiery steppe equivalent of 'poteen', Ireland's unique form of 'hooch'. Horse dung provides fuel for fires, while hides are used for clothing and the construction of the *yurt*. The latter was the precursor of the wigwam of the Native Americans, who in all probability were a descendant of Asian nomads who had migrated over the pre-glacial landbridges to the new pastures offered by the American continent.

Of course, the possession of horses, even in the age of the pick-up truck, confers mobility as well as a means of transport and communication, but in the instance of the Bashkir horses of Bashkiria, on the southern foothills of the Urals, even the thick coat hair serves a useful purpose. The Bashkir herds, living out in deep snow and the blizzard conditions of winter, when temperatures drop to between 30 and 40 °C below freezing (-22 to -40 °F), have developed a particularly thick, curled coat accompanied by a luxurious, protective growth of mane and tail. Combings from the coat are woven to make blankets and items of clothing, and American sources claim that such material can be used even by those usually allergic to horses, a condition, one imagines, that would be rare among the horse-people of Central Asia.

The American connection is of interest, since in the north-west of that country a 'Bashkir Curly', curly being an allusion to the coat, is registered as a breed! How the Bashkirs came to America is problematical. What is certain is that the American explanation is quite untenable. It postulates the arrival of the Bashkirs, along with their owners, over the landbridges of the Bering Strait prior to its disappearance at the end of the Ice Age. It is entirely possible that humans came into America by that route and possibly horses too, but the explanation takes no account of the proven fact that the horse became extinct on that continent some 8,000 years ago. There is no evidence at all that the horses brought to America by the Spanish in the sixteenth century had even a remote connection with those of the Bashkirian steppes!

The Bashkir herds are the traditional inhabitants of the Ural steppe lands but it was not until about 150 years ago that they obtained 'official' recognition as being integral to the local economy. Breeding centres were then established in 1845, to improve the stock, although the animals continued to be maintained in semi-feral conditions.

The improvement of the stock by the employment of selective breeding methods was made with the object of increasing the effective use of the horses for the purpose of agriculture, transport, and so on, but also, and just as importantly, to increase the productivity in respect of meat and milking potential. To this end meat processing factories and creameries for dairy produce have been established.

Bashkir mares, with their natural diet supplemented in the worst weather by a ration of the steppe-grown hay, have a surprisingly high milk yield. During a seven to eight-month lactation period an average yield of some 1,500 litres (330 gall) may be expected whilst the very best milkers may produce as much as 2,700 litres (550 gall).

The Bashkir is a wide-bodied, stocky animal of between 13 and 14h.h (132-142cm) standing on short, strong limbs and is, very necessarily, extraordinarily hardy. It is also noted for its powers of endurance and three Bashkirs, harnessed to a sledge *troika* fashion (i.e. in a triangle formed of a centre lead horse and two outriggers) is claimed to be able to cover over 75 miles a day.

Kazakh horses are kept in similar conditions and for much the same purpose, as well as their sub-types, the Adaev and Dzhabe and the Buryat of Siberia, which, not surprisingly in view of its inhospitable habitat, is covered with the same sort of long, thick hair as the Bashkir.

This head study of a Bashkir was made at the Kentucky

Horse Park which maintains a representative selection of many

horse and pony breeds. In America, the breed is termed Bashkir Curly

on account of the peculiar curled nature of the coat.

*The oldest of the British 'native' or Mountain and Moorland
breeds, is the Exmoor, which shares its wild, harsh habitat with the
red deer. There is little evidence of any significant outside influence on the
Exmoor ponies since the Bronze Age.*

A Unique Equine Grouping

No country has such a wealth of indigenous pony stock as Britain. There are, indeed, nine recognised native pony breeds which are often referred to as Mountain and Moorland ponies. The description, Mountain and Moorland, comes about because the original habitat of the ponies was on the wild, sparsely populated uplands of Britain, and in the case of the New Forest Pony, the rough moor and woodland environment of Hampshire's New Forest, once a royal hunting ground and still the largest unenclosed area in southern England.

The Highland and Shetland ponies of Scotland have their origins on the Western Isles and the Shetland Islands respectively, the latter lying some 100 miles north of the Scottish mainland.

The Fell ponies of northern England occupied the northern edge of the Pennines and the moorlands of Cumbria and Westmorland on the eastern side of Britain, while their neighbours, the related Dales ponies, belonged to the opposite side of the Pennine chain in the Upper Dales of Tyne, Allen, Wear and Tees in north Yorkshire. The Welsh breeds, both ponies and cobs, were and still are to be found all over the principality and continue to be put out to range the Welsh hills from Gwynedd and Clwyd in the north to the Brecons and the Gower Peninsula in the south.

Ireland's sole pony breed is the justly famous Connemara, which takes its name from that part of western Ireland bounded by Galway Bay to the south and facing the Atlantic Ocean on the west.

The south-west of England is home to the Dartmoor and the most ancient and purest of the native breeds, the Exmoor.

All these ponies evolved from the early forms of *Equus caballus* and the subsequent sub-types which developed from that base, and they did so long before the British Isles had separated from the European mainland.

Their development continued after the last landbridge from the Scilly Isles disappeared in the old Stone Age, about 15,000 BC. Thus for some 14,000 years, up to the Bronze Age, when trading ships were big enough to carry livestock, the native pony population developed largely in accordance with the environmental influence and without being subject to infusions of outside blood. As a result, and despite the inevitable crosses between the types, the British ponies maintained a more or less fixed character, and none more so than the Exmoor, whose habitat on the high plateau of Exmoor was as inaccessible as any.

None of the Mountain and Moorland breeds are truly feral although they can still be seen living in herd and family groups within the original habitat.

Of them all, there is little doubt that the Exmoor lives closest to the wild state and retains more of the 'wild' character than any other of the British native breeds.

In general terms, the best of the New Forest stock and the most commercially valuable, are bred at privately-owned studs, some of them close to the Forest itself. Nonetheless, large numbers of ponies are still kept in the New Forest under the 'Right of Common Pasture' enjoyed by the Commoners. The Forest stock certainly has a character formed as a result of its environment, but it is of such mixed origins that it cannot be compared to the Exmoor, which is unique in so many respects.

Exmoor, in the western part of Somerset, is the smallest and among the most wild and inhospitable of the British National Parks. The Moor supports herds of red deer as well as herds of pure-bred Exmoor ponies. The most important of these is the Anchor herd, formed by Sir Thomas Acland early in the nineteenth century following the deforestation and partial enclosure of Exmoor in 1818. These ponies are easily distinguished by the anchor brand mark on the near-side of the quarter. Other herds are marked with a herd number on the shoulder below the Exmoor Pony Society's star, a brand made only after the animals have passed a stringent examination for type, conformation, soundness and correct colouring.

Ponies of mixed breeding are also to be found on the Moor, as well as some inevitable scrub stock; that is, largely degenerate animals, the product of promiscuous breeding. The mixed stock can be seen on the commons of Withypool, Molland and Brendon, whilst the pure-bred herds are confined for the most part to the areas around Ashway Side, Winsford Hill, Codsend Moor and Cheriton Ridge.

The area is one of high rainfall and in winter climatic conditions are extremely harsh. The cold can be intense and conditions of deep, drifting snow are usual. Additionally the Moor is intersected with swift-running rivers flowing through the steep-sided valleys, known in England's West Country as combes.

The vegetation of the Moor comprises heather, rough grasses and bracken. The deer and the ponies eat the bracken shoots without ill effect, although they are poisonous to sheep, and in the winter they will paw up the bracken and cotton grass to get at the starch-filled tubers.

Because of its unique character and origins the Exmoor has been a fruitful source for scientific study. Both Professor Ebhardt of the Veterinary College at Hanover and Professor J G Speed at the Royal (Dick) Veterinary School at

The vegetation of the Moor includes large areas of bracken,

the young shoots of which are eaten with impunity by both the red deer

and the Exmoor ponies, although they are poisonous to sheep.

There are still small pure-bred herds of Dartmoor ponies
on the south-western moorlands of England, but most modern ponies
are bred on studs throughout the UK. The Dartmoor is, nonetheless, one
of the world's most elegant riding ponies.

Edinburgh carried out detailed studies of the breed which revealed a close connection between the Exmoor and equine remains of the Pleistocene period discovered in Alaska. From these it was possible to trace a trail through mainland Europe to the south-west of England and the Exmoor. In fact, the bone structure of the modern Exmoor matches in numerous details that of the remains of two million years ago: in particular there is a unique jaw formation not found in any other equine race. To cope with coarse feedstuffs a seventh molar tooth was developed in the lower jaw and it is retained in the modern pony.

The Exmoor is a strong, well-built, robust pony of no more than 12.3h.h (130cm) and stands on short, well-formed legs. The coat colours can be bay, brown or dun, in this instance a slate-coloured grey, without any white markings. There is a characteristic 'mealy' colouring round the eyes, muzzle and the inner flanks. Particular Exmoor features, which act to counter the effects of extreme cold and wet, are the hooded, 'toad' eye; the 'ice' tail, which has an additional thick, fan-like growth at the top, and the double-textured coat which provides a natural waterproof cover and is resistant to the most bitter winds. Interestingly, the Exmoor head is proportionately larger in comparison with that of other pony breeds, the only possible exception being the Shetland pony. The increased size allows the nasal passages to be longer so that cold air is warmed before entering the lungs.

The herds are 'gathered' once a year and driven to the owners' farms to be inspected and, if necessary, branded. The foals which are to be sold can also be separated off. The whole business takes up to a fortnight after which the herds are returned to the moor.

The 'gathering' is the sole point of contact with humans and as a result the Exmoor herds are wary of the latter's presence, either on foot or as members of a mounted group and will, indeed, become nervous at the approach of a large dog. Herds have been observed to react to the primitive 'wolf alert', which is rare and to all intents unknown in anything but wild stock. It occurs, for example, in the American Mustang which will behave in the same way if threatened by what are perceived as potential predators.

Under threat a group of ponies will take up a defensive position prompted, it may be assumed, by the activation of some atavistic memory. Enclosing the foals, the ponies form a tight circle, the adults facing inwards to present a wall of hind-feet ready to repulse any attack. This formation revolves slowly on its axis while the herd stallion faces the suspected danger with teeth and slashing fore-feet from outside the circle.

There is little or no evidence of any sustained outside influence on the breed since the Bronze Age when the Exmoor was used in chariots and acquired a peculiar conformational feature that was to persist for centuries. Early chariot harnesses were based on the ox yoke and the horses pulled the lightweight chariot from a broad strap fitted round their necks. As a result the animals developed a pronounced muscular bulge on the underside of the neck. Remarkably, the bulge was not entirely eradicated until the beginning of the century.

In Roman Britain the Exmoor became a saddle horse and is depicted in stone carvings of the second century as a very recognisable modern Exmoor, 'toad' eyes and all. Similar depictions of what are undoubtedly Exmoors appear on the Bayeux Tapestry illustrating the landing of William the Conqueror in Britain in 1066.

The Knight family of Simonsbath attempted to improve their Exmoor herds in the early years of the nineteenth century by introducing a Barb type stallion, but neither it, nor the later use of Welsh Cobs had any lasting effect on the stock.

Sir Thomas Acland, son of the founder of the Anchor herd, wrote that his father had some 500 head of wild Exmoor stock on the Moor in 1815 and mentioned the presence in the herds of a stallion called Katerfelto, a horse of either Arab or Spanish origin. The horse became something of a legend on the Moor. Although he was eventually captured, how he got to the Moor remains a mystery. What was settled was that he was not an Arab, for he was a dun horse with black points, a coat pattern that occurs in Spanish stock but never in the pure-bred Arabian.

Traditionally, the Exmoor is famous as a hunting pony and is still capable of carrying a grown man to hounds. William Youatt, the nineteenth-century authority, wrote in 1820 of 'a well-known sportsman' who rode an Exmoor and 'never felt such power and action in so small a compass.' The same gentleman, who weighed 14 stone (196lb), was reputed to have jumped a gate on the pony that stood some eight inches higher than his mount. Riding the same pony he claimed to have covered the 86 miles from Bristol to South Molton in less time than the fastest stagecoach of the day.

The Exmoor is notably independent by nature, but properly schooled makes a brilliant all-round pony for a keen child and is a courageous performer in harness. As a foundation for the breeding of competition horses, by using the Thoroughbred cross, the Exmoor is probably unsurpassed, handing on constitutional strength, hardiness, intelligence and that peculiar sagacity that contributes to the 'streetwise' quality of the pony breeds.

The natural habitat of the ponies of

the New Forest provides adequate, but never

abundant feed, so long as a limit is put on

the numbers of grazing stock.

Unhappily, the future of the Exmoor is far from being assured and should there be further enclosures of the natural habitat the ponies would be at risk. Already the Rare Breeds Survival Trust has expressed its anxiety by placing the breed in Category 1, indicating that numbers have reached a dangerously low level. Indeed, there may be as few as 500 pure-bred Exmoors worldwide. A contributing factor to the alarming decrease in numbers is the seeming inability of the breed to thrive, or at any rate retain type, away from their natural environment on the Moor.

To the east of the Moor lies Hampshire's New Forest, through which for centuries the principal routes ran to the west and the old English capital of Winchester. The Forest Law of King Canute proclaimed in Winchester in 1016, makes it clear that ponies grazed in the forest at this time along with cattle and pigs, and the present day Commoners, to whom the ponies belong, continue to run their stock in the Forest.

The body responsible for the administration of the New Forest and for the welfare and improvement of its stock, which includes the control and inspection of stallions, is the Court of Verderers, half of which is composed of members elected by the Commoners. The Verderers employ three Agisters to carry out the day to

Exmoor ponies are easily recognisable by their distinctive colouring, which includes the typical 'mealy' muzzle.

36

day management and their duties include tail-marking the ponies; cutting the tail hair in a way that makes it easy to identify the ponies and to relate them to the districts in which they graze.

There are regular sales of Forest ponies held at Beaulieu Road throughout the year, for which the ponies must be rounded up, tail-marked and branded. These 'pony drifts' organised by the Agisters and carried out by mounted Commoners, are a highlight of the New Forest year and like a Wild West round-up, call for hard, bold riding that is not without an element of danger. Colt-hunting, when designated animals need to be captured, is another exercise undertaken by the Commoners and is roughly the equivalent of the Western rodeo event of calf-wrestling, two riders acting in concert to bring the colt down and get a rope round its neck.

The isolated habitat of the Exmoor pony played a large part in maintaining the purity of that breed, but the Forest ponies have had no such protection from outside influences. The accessibility of the Forest has resulted in the introduction of a bewildering variety of outside stock. Very often animals were put into the Forest with the deliberate and praiseworthy intention of effecting improvements, but such a diversity of breeds made it difficult to fix the type in respect of height, colour and conformational features.

The first recorded attempt to upgrade the Foresters, as they are called, was in 1208 when 18 Welsh mares were put out. The Welsh influence was a persistent one through the breed's history, but Highlands, Fells, Dales, Dartmoors, Exmoors, Arabs, Barbs and Thoroughbreds have all played their part. Lord Lucas, the first chairman of the New Forest breed society and a great, if unconventional, improver of the Forest stock, even went so far as to put out a Basuto stallion which he had brought back from the Boer War, in which conflict he had lost a leg while with the New Forest Scouts, all of whom were mounted on New Forest ponies.

Some diversity of type still exists in the New Forest pony, but overall distinctive common features are now clearly discernible in the modern stock.

Lord Arthur Cecil, friend and contemporary of Lucas and an 'improver' in the same enthusiastic mould, attributed the eventual emergence of a distinctive type of Forester to the pervading influence of the environment, although the process was certainly accelerated by the breed Society's ban on further out-crosses, made in the 1930s. Cecil wrote of that 'mysterious power of nature to grind down and assimilate all these types to the one most suited to the land', and that power is certainly exemplified in the character of the Forest pony.

There is a height variation in the Forest-bred ponies, which may be as small as 12-12.2h.h (122-127cm), whilst the stud-bred animals reach the maximum permitted height of 14.2h.h (147cm). All colours are to be found, but piebald, skewbald and creams are not acceptable for entry into the Society's stud book.

The action of the Foresters is without doubt very distinctive and has been formed as a result of the ground conditions in the Forest. They are naturally sure-footed but the length of stride is unusual in pony breeds. Without much doubt the canter is the best pace and it is the one, of course, best suited for crossing open moorland. Because of the length and freedom of the movement, the New Forest pony, with the Connemara, is probably the most commercially viable of the British native breeds. It is fast, versatile and has the scope that allows it to excel in modern competitive events, particularly as a cross-country performer.

Occasionally, the heads may be large and lacking in pony character, and some of the Forest-bred stock tend to fall away in the line of the quarters. Nonetheless, almost all have the well-sloped shoulder which allows for long, low strides and is the hallmark of the riding pony. Temperamentally, the Forester is docile, highly intelligent and possessed of common sense. Foresters are accustomed to traffic passing through the Forest, they move freely round and through the villages and because of their regular contact with humans they are more easily handled, less nervous and perhaps less sharp, or cunning, than some of the wilder native breeds.

There is another side to this trusting nature, however, for many ponies, encouraged by titbits given by visitors, are injured in road accidents and do, indeed, present a driving hazard in the Forest.

Whilst the feed offered in the Forest environment has never been abundant, it is sufficient so long as the grazing stock is kept within acceptable limits. The ponies feed principally on the purple moor grass, found round the Forest bogs, and on other coarse grasses, sedge, rushes, brambles, tree shoots and gorse tips, which are particularly favoured. In some areas the ponies have adapted so as to consume this prickly food without discomfort, growing wiry 'moustaches' on the upper lip and sometimes having a rudimentary beard protecting the lower jaw.

Today, concern is being expressed by welfare societies about the management of the Forest ponies and the numbers kept in relation to diminished areas of grazing that are incapable of their support. There is little doubt that some owners are failing in their responsibilities and there has certainly been harsh criticism made of the Forest's management in recent years, but the underlying problem is one of too many ponies on too little grazing.

Large numbers of New Forest ponies are still kept in the Forest under the 'Right of Common Pasture'. Because of the Forest's accessibility, the breed is of very mixed origin, nonetheless, modern stock exhibit clearly discernible common features and character.

New Forest foals are attractive and appealing, and quickly
become accustomed to the presence of humans. The Exmoor (opposite)
is especially distinctive among the British native breeds. The head is larger
in comparison with those of other breeds, and is noticeable for the mealy
colouring round the hooded, 'toad' eyes and the muzzle.

HORSES OF THE SEA

The beauty of the Camargue horses lies in the silky white coat and their overwhelming impression of courage and spirit when in movement.

The white horses of the Camargue, inhabiting the inhospitable watery wastes of the Rhône Delta in the south of France, are as ancient a breed as the Exmoors, and like them have a unique character. Their environment is harsh and even savage. In summer the hot, searing sun bakes the ground until it cracks, whilst in winter the land is covered with a winding sheet of icy water. The whole is dominated by the tearing *mistral*, the salt-laden wind which stunts the vegetation supporting the *manades*, the herds of semi-wild horses that share this place with the aggressive, black fighting bulls and which like them are the very essence of the Camargue. The people of this unpromising swampland are as independent as their horses and cattle and fiercely proud of what they call 'the most noble conquered territory of man'.

Today, much of the Camargue has been drained to allow the cultivation of rice and vines, and tourism plays an increasingly important part in the economy. The 17,000 acre lagoon of Etang de Vacares, for instance, is now a nature reserve attracting many thousands of visitors, a proportion of whom will observe the wonderful variety of wildlife from the backs of the Camargue horses.

Nonetheless, it is the horses and the fighting bulls that remain central to the tradition of the Camargue, and provide much of its spectacle and romance as well. Every year thousands attend the festivals in the principal town of Sainte Marie de la Mer to see the gaily dressed *gardians*, the keepers of the bulls and the French equivalent of the cowboy, galloping the bulls through the streets on the white 'horses of the sea' and taking part in fierce, almost elemental, mounted games.

The Camargue, like most horses kept in natural, semi-wild conditions, is incredibly tough and hardy, and is possessed of its own particular vigour. In its own habitat it rarely needs to be shod and subsists satisfactorily enough on the coarse diet of tough, salt grasses, reeds and saltwort that it shares with the black cattle. The breed is considered to have been indigenous to the area from pre-history although its early origins remain something of a mystery, despite extensive research which has resulted in it being recognised as a specific French breed by the National Stud authorities since 1968, when a breeders' association was formed.

During the nineteenth century, prehistoric remains of horses, estimated as being about 50,000 years old, were excavated at Solutré, a village in the Charolais region. The skeletons, in terms of proportion and other detail, resemble closely those of the present-day Camargue. Much later in time, there is the evidence of the remarkable cave pictures at Lascaux and Niaux which were probably executed in about 15,000 BC. Some of these bear a strong resemblance to the Camargue horses.

Inevitable influences on the region's indigenous equine stock would have been made by Asian and Mongol horses, the mounts of invading Ostro-Goths and Vandals who passed this way in their forays into Europe. Certainly the powerful genes of the Barb horses, brought into Europe by the Moorish conquerors of the Iberian Peninsula in the eighth century, would have made their mark, and there is evidence of the powerful Barb blood in the appearance of the modern Camargue. That association is reinforced by the tradition of bull-raising, the style of the *gardians* and the saddlery and equipment which they use. It is, indeed, identical to that first developed in Spain and Portugal during the long Moorish occupation and still in use in those countries today. From that point, however, the isolation of the *manades* has ensured purity of descent and there is no evidence of other outcrosses.

Despite the romance of the Camargue, immortalised in verse and legend, and conjured up in the vision of pure white horses galloping in the mist of the sea spray, the Camargue horse is not a very prepossessing equine specimen. Indeed, its peculiarly silky white coat, so often likened to the foam of the sea, is probably its most attractive asset. Otherwise, there is, indeed, a 'primitive' look about the horse, which is by no means masked by the Barb influence.

The head is inclined to be heavy and coarse whilst the neck is short and the shoulders upright. But, on closer inspection, the horses are remarkably deep-bodied with strong backs and limbs, even though the quarter, like that of the old-type Barb, slopes downward from the croup. There is no argument about their stamina and endurance nor about their high courage, agility and in-bred ability to face and work the unpredictable Camargue cattle like a sheepdog controlling a flock of sheep.

The Camargue horse rarely exceeds 15h.h (152cm) and is noted for its exceptional longevity. The coat colour is always white, the foals, of course, being born black, and the action is peculiarly distinctive.

The Camargue horses, despite the upright shoulders which do not usually allow much length of stride, have an exceptionally long, high-stepping walk, moving in that pace with great activity. Conversely, the trot is very short, stilted and uncomfortable to ride, for which reason it is not much employed. But, in compensation, the canter and gallop are strong and free.

Despite the inevitable encroachments on the environment, which have, indeed, been made with some degree of sensitivity, there seems for the moment no reason to fear for the future of the horses of the sea.

The Camargue stallions can be aggressive in driving off intruders with designs on their own group of mares, but like all horses, they are not by nature territorial animals.

CAMARGUE HORSE

The diet available in the salt marshlands of the Camargue

is sparse by most standards, but the horses subsist well enough

on the reeds and tough grasses, enlivened occasionally, one

presumes, by a feed of poppies.

Despite the paucity of feed, shared with the black

fighting bulls of the region, the incredibly tough Camargue horses thrive in

the Rhône salt lands which are forever dominated by the tearing mistral,

the salt wind of the 'most noble conquered territory of man.'

THE CAMARGUE

Even the brackish water is acceptable to the hardy,

uncompromising horses of the Camargue, whose presence

complements the stark beauty of their environment.

The Asturçon pony, still found in the mountains of
Asturia in northern Spain, derives from a common Celtic root and
has existed in Europe since before the Ice Age (c. 10,000 BC). It bears
a striking resemblance to the ponies of Exmoor and Dartmoor.

An Iberian Legacy

Further south from the Camargue, the Pyrenees, dividing France from Spain, are the home of little known horses and ponies whose origin is no less a source of conjecture than those of the Camargue. The three principal breeds are the Landais, once a semi-wild pony and probably much influenced by Tarpan blood, which ran in the wooded areas of the Landes region north of the frontier; the Basque Pottock, which until relatively recent times was regarded as being wild or, at best, semi-wild, and the Ariègois, the mountain horse of Andorra and the eastern edges of the Pyrenean chain.

The Landais is now thoroughly domesticated and the little Pottock hardly less so, but the latter, along with the Ariègois may still be kept in semi-feral conditions. Both the last two excel as sure-footed pack animals under the most difficult conditions and for that reason both were used to carry contraband, after the inherent tradition of the region, right up to World War II, and perhaps after.

The old breed of Ariègois, unadulterated by the crosses with heavy horse breeds that have been practiced in the lower reaches of the Department of Ariège, are still to be found in a semi-feral state in the fastnesses of the high *soulanes* around Andorra on the border with Spain. The breed is a solid black in colour and very like the British Fell pony in character. Some of the Cro-Magnon cave paintings at Niaux are certainly recognisable as Camargue horses but others, just as surely, depict the black Ariègois with the characteristic beard which accompanies the thick, wiry winter coat and the heavy, protective mane and tail. Not surprisingly these mountain horses are impervious to the most severe climatic conditions, but they are not resistant to heat and have to be sheltered from the summer sun.

The indigenous pony stock of Spain and Portugal are even less well-known, although they are, in fact, of special interest in the equine development. In the north of Spain, in the mountainous region of Asturia, a breed of strong, active ponies has survived for thousands of years without being much affected by outside influences, although they are now significantly reduced in number. They are called Asturçon and belong to the same Celtic strain as the ponies of Dartmoor and Exmoor, to which they bear a striking resemblance. There is little recorded information about the Asturçon, but there is no doubt that it was the mount of the Asturian horsemen (themselves of Celtic origin) who formed part of the Roman auxiliary cavalry.

Up to 80 years ago the Asturçon existed in large numbers, living in wild herds in their largely inaccessible mountain habitat. Today the herds have gone. Some however, are kept in a semi-feral state and about 200 animals are registered in a stud book formed by members of the local Wild Life Society. Otherwise, the Asturçon is finding employment as a child's pony as a result of the recent formation of a Spanish Pony Club. Indeed, a 13.2h.h (137cm) Asturçon won the Spanish Showjumping Championship in its height division only a couple of years ago and these new competitive activities may well give encouragement to the maintenance and extension of this valuable pony stock.

The Sorraia pony is probably even older and is one of the very rare links with the earliest horses of pre-history. It descends principally from the Tarpan but there is also an element of the Asiatic Wild Horse in the background. The forebears of the Sorraia and its close relation the Garrano, which stems from the same primitive root, were most probably the first equines to be domesticated in Europe. If that is so, and there is no argument to the contrary, then it was these ponies, when crossed with the Barb horses of North Africa that were responsible for the Spanish Horse, whose prepotent blood was to be a major influence on the world's equine population until well into the eighteenth century.

For thousands of years Iberia's indigenous stock was distributed over the whole Peninsula. It is only latterly that diminished numbers have become concentrated in particular areas. The habitat of the Sorraia has become the plains lying between the Sor and Raia rivers (running through both Portugal and Spain), whilst the Garrano or Minho is raised in the more fertile mountain valleys of Garranos do Minho and Traz dos Montes in the north of Portugal. The latter has been a subject for improvement by the Portuguese Ministry of Agriculture and now bears little resemblance to its primitive ancestors. It has become a refined, quality pony with a neat, pretty head, that as a result of continued infusions of Arab blood, has a noticeably concave profile.

The Sorraia has been less affected and many reveal their Tarpan antecedents in their conformation and coat colour. They have certainly been improved by out-crossing and the modern Sorraia is far more attractive than its predecessors. Some, indeed, are virtually miniature versions (12-13h.h, 122-132cm) of the Iberian Horse which today goes under the name of Lusitano, Andalucian or Alter-Real, even though all those breeds spring from a common root.

The Sorraia of 50 years ago was an obvious Tarpan derivative and even now the characteristics persist. There is still evidence of the upright shoulder, the straight back, the large head and convex profile and of the coat colours also. The deer grey colour is apparent, with its peculiar short wiry hair, and there is still the

The Sorraia pony is indigenous to the Iberian Peninsula. This horse has been fitted with a bell by the Portuguese National Stud, to help find it on its range.

characteristically primitive dun, as well as a dullish, palomino yellow. Dark points (i.e. black legs, mane and tail) are not unusual, along with eel stripes down the back and sometimes barred, zebra markings on the lower legs. The ears are long and set unusually high in the head and, as in the primitive horses, they are tipped with black hair. Like its ancestors, the modern Sorraia is incredibly hardy. It can survive in conditions of extreme cold or heat and is able to subsist satisfactorily on the poorest soils and the most sparse forage.

Before agricultural mechanisation, the local 'cowboys' working in the plains of the Sor used the ponies for a variety of jobs, and ponies were kept in an almost wild state. Thereafter numbers declined and the stock were allowed to degenerate. To prevent the disappearance of the Sorraia and the loss of a valuable part of the equine gene bank, the late Dr Ruy d'Andrade, a world authority associated with some of the most significant studies in equine development, kept a small, pure Sorraia herd in the natural state and this was continued after his death by his son Fernando. This herd proved a principal factor in the conservation and subsequent improvement of the breed, and whilst a wild herd no longer exists the Sorraia is still kept in semi-feral conditions as well as in a controlled domesticated state.

CHINCOTEAGUE PONY

ISLAND HORSES

Chincoteague ponies live on the national park island of Assateague, off the coast of Virginia, USA. Most probably, they derive from stock that strayed or was abandoned there in the seventeenth century.

Sable Island, lying some 100 miles off the east coast of Nova Scotia, is as unlikely a place as any to find wild horses. It is, in fact, no more than a sandbank approximately 30 miles long (48km) and 1 mile wide (1.6km). There are no trees and the vegetation is limited to low shrubs, coarse dune grasses and wild pea plants growing near the water's edge. It is often covered in sea fogs and its shape changes constantly under the onslaught of the fierce Atlantic storms. The approaches to the islands are treacherous and over the centuries have taken a heavy toll of shipping blown off course or attempting a landing. It appears on the maps as Sable Island, the Dark Island, but to seafarers it was also known as the 'Graveyard of the Atlantic'.

Astonishingly, this inhospitable strip of land has been inhabited, and has supported domestic animals since mid-way through the sixteenth century when Portuguese expeditions to the Canadian shores put cattle and pigs on the island, which they called Santa Cruz. It has been suggested that horses were put ashore also, but there is no evidence to support this theory and the story of horses swimming to land from shipwrecks has to be regarded with some suspicion. The number of breeds supposedly influenced by, or attributed to, shipwrecked equines (from the Spanish Armada that sailed against England, for example) range from Connemaras, New Forests and Dartmoors to the horses of the Indian sub-continent and Indonesia. These stories may provide convenient, romantic and superficial explanations for the presence or the development of an equine group but they have to be seen as mythical rather than factual.

The Company of New France was formed in 1627 when Isaac de Razilly was appointed Lieutenant General of New France, called 'Canada', and Governor of Acadia. He made landfall at La Havre, Nova Scotia (then La Hève, Acadia) in 1632. His small fleet of three ships carried prospective settlers, seeds, tools, livestock and, importantly, horses of Norman or Norman-Breton stock from the principal horse-raising area of France. At that time Sable Island was supporting some 800 head of cattle which the French slaughtered for hides and meat, but there is still no evidence about the introduction of horses, even though they were to hand. Over 100 years later in 1738 Andrew Le Mercier, a Huguenot minister from Boston, applied to rent land on the island for the purpose of settlement, the raising of cattle and the hunting of seals. Fifteen years later when Le Mercier advertised his holdings on the Island for sale, he stated, 'When I took possession of the Island, there were no four-footed creatures upon it but a few foxes, some red and some black, now there are I suppose about 90 sheep, between 20 or 30 horses, including colts, stallions and breeding mares, about 30 or 40 cows, tame and wild, and 40 hogs.'

By this time, Acadia was under English rule and had been re-named New Scotland (Nova Scotia) and there had been imports of English horses, probably early 'Thoroughbreds' as well as the influence of the Spanish-based stock, descendants of the horses brought to the Americas by the *conquistadores*. All these elements would have bred with the Acadian horses.

Early in the nineteenth century, several small herds had become established on the Island. In 1801, James Morris, the first superintendent of the Island estimated that there were some 90 horses there. These horses were wild '... of a middling size,' he wrote '... and three-quarters of them bay and the other various coloured. They are very wild and fleet and have in general a very handsome trot and canter.'

Morris, with great difficulty, managed to capture some of them and they were later broken to saddle when they proved to be extraordinarily sure-footed, very fast and able to go over rough ground all day.

An observer writing of them in 1885 stated that, 'The horses trot, jump, gallop, paddle, rack, prance, shuffle, and waltz ...' and he paid tribute to their speed, hardiness and ability to jump gulches of 15 feet or more when they were engaged in rounding up the wild stock.

Between 1884 and 1911 under the capable management of Robert J Boutilier, the most successful of the Island's administrators, the land was much improved by the extensive planting of tussock grass, clovers and other seeds as well as thousands of saplings and shrubs. At the same time imported stallions, as well as some mares, were put out with the horse herds. There were a number of Thoroughbreds, a Morgan cross, a Standardbred trotter, Hackneys of the old Norfolk Roadster stamp, the then popular Thoroughbred/Clydesdale cross and an experiment to increase size and weight was attempted, not very successfully, by the introduction of two heavy Belgian Draught horses.

Imported, 'tame' stallions needed to be tough, aggressive sorts, for they had to contend with the wild stallions in fights to secure their territory and the overlordship of their mare band. Some were simply run out of town whilst others could not withstand the climate and maintain the condition needed to look after their mares and keep off their young rivals. Those that did adapt, however, proved their value by increasing the herds' numbers and the quality of the stock, much of which was

The Sable Island horses descend from stock put out on this Atlantic sandbank, off Nova Scotia, in the eighteenth century. There is no evidence of a definitive fixed type, but they are noted for their speed, agility and endurance.

rounded up regularly to be sent to the mainland and even to the West Indies.

Although there is no fixed type of Sable Island horse the environment itself imposes its own common features on the stock, particularly in respect of hardiness, stamina and the peculiar handiness of the animals under difficult conditions.

Today, there are some 2-300 horses on the Island, divided into small herds under their own stallions and keeping, very largely, to their own established piece of territory. The colour is predominantly bay, followed by chestnut, but there are some palominos and some blacks and browns.

Descriptions of the horses vary from one observer to another, but Dr D A Welsh of the Department of Biology, Dalhousie University, who made exhaustive studies in the late 1970s, wrote that 'a typical Sable Island stands about 14h.h (142cm) ... In appearance they most closely resemble the Barb of North Africa.' Other descriptions are critical of the conformation, noting the characteristically drooping quarter and the common head. In fact, both these features were to be found in the North African Barb of the type used exclusively by the French Spahi regiments of Morocco and acknowledged as one of the toughest horses in the world.

Sable Island horses are still rounded up for export
to the mainland, and in times past there was considerable
trade with the plantations of the West Indies.

Whatever the source of comment there is universal agreement about the versatility, speed, courage, strength and powers of endurance of the Sable Island horses.

Daniel Welsh concluded that '... the unique characteristics of these horses as a whole are undoubtedly due to exposure to the rigours of the environment over many generations without human interference.' As such, the Sable Island herds represent a valuable gene bank which can be dipped into to reinvigorate more artificially created types and breeds. On that score alone it is very desirable that they should be preserved.

Seven hundred miles to the south of Nova Scotia there are more island horses whose origins are far less documented than those of Sable Island. Wild stock still inhabit the islands of Chincoteague and Assateague which lie just off the coast of Virginia. Most of the 200 or so ponies live on Assateague, now a National Park, which until the unusually severe storms of 1933 was connected to the mainland. The islands were owned and managed by the Chincoteague Volunteer Fire Department which is responsible for the ponies' welfare. However, in 1943 a conservation agency, the Federal Fish and Wildlife Service, was introduced to the 9,000 acre (3,600ha) island of Assateague to encourage and protect the wonderfully varied wild fowl and seabird population. The needs of the ponies, however, were not entirely compatible with those of the birds and when the FFWS fenced off its 'government-built pools' in an effort to preserve the wild fowl habitat the action produced an immediate conflict of interest between the needs of the birds and those of the ponies. The fencing of the pools confined the ponies to a small, low-lying and marshy part of the island and reduced the available grazing areas substantially. Just as significantly, it denied the animals access to the sea where they went in summer to avoid the hordes of biting mosquitoes. Because of the enclosures many ponies were trapped by the exceptionally high storm tides of 1962 and were drowned. A measure of compromise has since been reached and the fortunes of the ponies and their future development has largely been secured by the weight of public opinion brought about by the publicity given by a book, *Misty of Chincoteague*, written by Marguerite Henry, and the 20th Century Fox film, *Misty*, which was made subsequently.

Marguerite Henry's book for children was written as early as 1947 after she had bought a week-old Chincoteague foal on a visit to the annual sales held on the Chincoteague island. Each year on Pony Penning Days, at the end of July, the Fire Department rounds up the stock on Assateague and swims them over the channel that separates the two islands. Proceeds from the sale of young stock go to defray the cost of managing the herd.

The involvement of the Fire Department in the island stock dates from the 1920s, and until then the existence of these wild herds was generally unknown. Even now their origin remains a mystery. The most likely explanation is that the herds derive from stock that strayed in early colonial times, and that implies some background of the pervasive Spanish/Barb blood introduced by the *conquistadores*. Of course, there has to be a tale of a sixteenth-century shipwreck of a vessel carrying horses from North Africa to Peru, but like all such stories it is totally unsupported by evidence and is best disregarded.

Unlike the horses of Sable Island, the Chincoteague stock cannot be regarded as being so genetically valuable. In earlier years the animals of the islands, whose height even today is not much over 12h.h (122cm), were no more than stunted, scrub *horses*, rather than ponies, which have their own particular character. They were degenerate in respect of bone, substance and structure as a result of in-breeding combined with a less than generous environment of sandy, salt-laden marshes bereft of essential minerals and providing no more than minimal feed of the poorest quality. Of necessity the animals adapted to these conditions and the rigours of the climate but were otherwise ill-fitted to fulfil any practical purpose. To redress the balance, and to retain the obvious constitutional strength, outside blood was sensibly introduced as a means of upgrading the quality of the herds. Welsh ponies featured strongly in the enterprise and some Shetlands were also used, but probably the greatest influence was that of the American Pinto, a part-coloured horse whose coat pattern is now much in evidence in the modern Chincoteague. The introduction of the Pinto was, indeed, the most logical to make, since the Pintos derive from the same Spanish stock which provide the base for the Chincoteague, and on that account are likely to be more genetically compatible than anything else.

Appreciation of the Chincoteague is likely, perhaps, to be more inspired by sentimentality than by knowledgeable assessment, but it has resulted in the conservation of an interesting equine group and there is now a market for the stock as children's ponies.

*Until the 1920s when the Chincoteague Fire Department
assumed responsibility for the island stock, the Chincoteague herds had
suffered considerable degeneration caused by poor feed and in-breeding.
Since then stock has been improved by the addition of Welsh ponies,
Shetlands and some Pinto blood.*

The vegetation of Sable Island is pretty much limited to
shrubs, coarse dune grasses and the pea plants that grow along the
water's edge, but the horses thrive on this fare and have developed
remarkable stamina and hardiness.

There are 2-300 head of stock on Sable Island today,
living in small herds under dominant stallions. Because of
their unique character they are regarded as a valuable gene
bank well worth preserving.

The scarcity of good food and running water
contributed to the earlier degeneration of the Chincoteague
stock, but the habitat nonetheless ensured the survival of none but
the toughest and most adaptable.

*It once seemed likely that the sun would set forever
on the Mustang herds, but now public opinion has ensured the
survival of America's wild horses.*

MUSTANGS AND BRUMBIES

Less than a hundred years ago it was estimated that over a million wild or semi-wild horses inhabited the western states of America. The state of Texas, for instance, still abounds with place names derived from the presence of wild horse herds. It has no less than twenty-seven places named Mustang Creek as well as numerous Horse Hollows, a town called Wild Horse and the Wild Horse Desert.

Mustang is a corruption of *Mesteno*, a word which, in fact, refers to horses that escaped or strayed from their supervised range and reverted to the wild state. They were not therefore truly wild horses, and should in theory be considered as *feral* animals. They originated with the cattle ranching settlements established by the early Spanish settlers in the American south-west, settlements which by the early seventeenth century were supporting considerable numbers of horses. A percentage of this stock became feral and, indeed, as early as 1579 there were herds of such horses in north central Mexico that were even then spreading northwards in large numbers.

These horses were, of course, from Spanish strains which at that time, and for many years to come, strongly reflected the influence of the Barb. They would usually not have been more than 14h.h (142cm) and no particular coat colour was predominant.

It was the availability of horses that altered the whole concept of life for the Native Americans and made them into the last of the world's 'horse-people'. Moreover, they were just as integral to the reality of the American West, for they were caught and broken in rough and ready fashion by professional 'bronco-busters' to provide mounts for the cowboys working the huge cattle herds. Bronco (or *broncho*) again comes from the Spanish. It means 'wild' or 'unruly' and is in some parts synonymous with 'Mustang'.

By the 1970s the herds were much depleted by the deprivations made by hunters and the demands of a meat market created, largely, by the pet-food manufacturers. At that time there were probably no more than 17-18,000 horses distributed over the nine western states. The survivors pulled back into the less accessible areas, particularly in Montana and Wyoming, and these became wild horse refuges with the animals being protected by law as an endangered species.

Just as effective as the law itself was the formation of protection and welfare societies by enthusiasts determined to conserve a valuable equine heritage and to

69

promote the future of the Mustang stock by making the public aware of the problems and dangers involved in its survival.

Some of these societies were straightforward welfare groups that are still active in legislative activities designed to protect the animals and preserve their natural range; others are concerned with research projects and some give practical help in the field by maintaining water supplies and providing essential minerals, like salt, for the Mustang stock. One of these societies, the National Mustang Association, was comprised of members who were originally 'Mustangers', the men who chased and captured wild horses. Now the poachers turned gamekeepers are dedicated to preserving their natural habitat and perpetuating the Mustang strains.

The pioneer of the Mustang support groups was Robert Brislawn, then of the Cayuse Ranch in Oshoto, Wyoming. In 1957 he formed the Spanish Mustang Registry, aimed specifically at perpetuating the old Spanish strains of both Barb and Andalucian type whose ancestors had gone feral 400 years before. 'We're trying to restore a breed, not create one,' said Brislawn, and he operated his Registry on the strictest procedural lines, refusing to enter horses that because of outcrossing, did not come within the laid-down guidelines in respect of character and appearance.

In the 1960s the American Mustang Association was formed and in the early 1970s the Spanish Barb Breeders Association. The former sought to preserve and promote the American Mustang '... through registration and an intelligent breeding programme,' whilst the latter was concerned with the restoration of the 'true Spanish Barb horse' based on documented descriptions made between the fifteenth and eighteenth centuries.

The effect of these societies, whatever their primary objective, has been to increase the awareness of America to what is to all intents a unique genetic heritage and, in the end, to obtain the powerful support of public opinion in protecting the future of the Mustang herds.

The only concentration of feral stock approaching in numbers and character that of the western states of America, is the Brumby population of Australia, and it has not fared nearly so well as its American equivalent, possibly because it has not attracted the same measure of conservationist support.

Horses were not introduced to Australia until 1788 when the first group of animals to be imported from the Cape of Good Hope landed in Sydney Cove on 26 January of that year. The modern Australian Stock Horse derives from those and later imports, which included both Arabians and Thoroughbreds.

It is unlikely that this Mustang mare and foal will end up

in a pet-food can, but in the 1930s, over 100,000 Mustangs

a year were slaughtered for this purpose alone.

The zebra stripes on the legs of this Montana
Mustang, a feature often accompanying a dun coat coloration, denotes
descent from the early Spanish horses brought to the Americas
by the sixteenth-century conquistadores.

Within 40 years of the landing at Sydney Cove the forerunner of the Stock Horse, the Australian Waler, which was bred principally in the colony of New South Wales, had evolved as what one authority described as being '... probably the best saddle horse in the World.' (R S Summerhays, *Observer's Book of Horses and Ponies* 1968).

Summerhays was referring to the period between Waterloo (1815) and the Crimean War (1854), and in the context of the cavalry remount. During World War I the Waler consolidated its enviable reputation when Australia provided over 120,000 horses for the allied forces, many of them serving in Allenby's victorious Desert Mounted Corps, which, in one of the world's classic cavalry operations, routed the Turkish army in Palestine during 1917-18.

The Waler, like its more refined successor the Australian Stock Horse, was a versatile, all-round working horse on the huge Australian sheep stations. It stood between 15 and 16h.h (152-163cm) and although not exceptionally fast it was enormously agile, both enduring and hardy, as well as being able to tolerate very high temperatures.

Horses of this sort were the ancestors of the wild Brumby, which had its origin in the years following the Australian Gold Rush of 1851 when horses strayed from the early mining settlements and ran loose in the rough, scrub country. Within a hundred years the Brumby herds had multiplied over and over again, to a point where they had become a serious nuisance. The thousands of horses impinging on the range of domestic stock soon became a real threat to the latter's grazing even on the huge acreage of the average Australian station. Increasingly, the stockmen, anxious to protect their animals from the depredations of the wild horses, looked upon them as vermin to be destroyed by all available means.

For many years the pet-food industry had encouraged the hunting of the Brumbies, and the shooting of wild horses had become an acceptable weekend sport for many Australians. By the 1960s, however, a major culling operation had begun which provoked worldwide condemnation and caused the Australian authorities great, and not wholly undeserved embarrassment.

The horses were pursued and shot in thousands by trigger-happy hunters from jeeps, light aircraft and helicopters. 8,000 horses were killed in this way in an area some 700 miles west of Brisbane. Elsewhere, a similar number were exterminated and on one property over 9,000 horses were shot. Killing on this scale took place wherever there was a concentration of Brumbies and even now, 30 years on, the controversy is far from dead.

There is little doubt that the huge Brumby herds deteriorated in type and quality as a result of an environment that was unable to sustain such numbers, but they also developed an uncanny instinct for survival, frequently outwitting their pursuers. Furthermore, the self-reliant Brumby is just as tough and hardy as any of its predecessors.

Caught up and properly handled there is no reason why they should not make useful saddle horses, despite their inherent wildness, but whilst Australians have an adequate supply of good quality domestic horses any significant move towards utilising the Brumby stock is unlikely.

The Brumbies of the Australian outback are descended from horses which strayed from the early mining settlements.

The Brumby herds, that multiplied alarmingly, caused
significant encroachment upon the domestic range. This resulted in a
massive culling operation in the 1960s that often had little regard for
humanity. Despite the culling, the tough, wary and self-reliant
Brumby still inhabits rough scrub country in large numbers.

Mustang stallions can be fiercely possessive about their mares. They certainly exert a dominant influence, but family groups are usually under the leadership of an older matriarch. In terms of conformation many wild horses are more than acceptable and the heads are often handsome.

*By the late 1950s Mustang herds like this one were hard to
find and the wild horse faced extinction. Twenty years on, the wild horse
population was estimated to be no more than 16,000, whereas it had
been upwards of two million a century before.*

Young male Mustangs that have still to collect

together their own group of mares, often live in bachelor

groups separate from the main herd.

Wild horse stock, breeding in natural conditions, usually
have higher fertility levels than domestic horses. These Mustang mares
will probably foal annually through their breeding span.

Mustang and Foal

The sand plains of Garub in Africa's Southern
Namib Desert are the home of the only grouping of wild horses
in the continent. This herd numbers about 250 and is of predominantly
Thoroughbred type. It is thought they are descendants of the stud
founded by Baron von Wolf before World War I.

Australian Brumbies become infinitely resourceful

in their struggle for survival and adapt easily to varied terrain,

even developing the ability to dig for water.

Mustangs indulging in mutual grooming. Tactile
signals of this sort play an important role in equine relationships as
part of the language of communication.

This study of a wild Mustang captures the very
spirit of the wild horse saga and perhaps also of Velma Johnston,
'Wild Horse Annie', whose persistence and determination resulted
in the passing of the first federal legislation, the
'Save the Mustang' bill of 1959.

Today, the Mustang herds of Wyoming are safe from the
mechanised and airborne pursuit which had decimated their numbers,
before public opinion ensured protective legislation.

ASSES OF THE WILDERNESS

A group of Mountain zebra at Etjo, Namibia. At one time the whole of southern Africa teemed with huge zebra herds, but today only three species survive.

Wild asses, often called Onager and in scientific parlance termed hemionid (half-ass), can still be found in Western Asia, particularly in Mongolia and on the Tibetan plateau, as well as in the arid desert areas of India's Rann of Kutch. However, their numbers, like those of the Indian tigers and the rhinos, have been seriously depleted by hunting, whilst the Persian Onager (*Equus hemionus onager*), the 'wild ass' of the Bible, is almost certainly extinct in the wild.

The word hemionid comes from the Greek and was used to describe an animal having the nature and characteristics of *both* horse and ass. It does not mean that the animal is a cross between the two, as in the instance of the mule, although that is often the interpretation.

Whilst belonging to the genus *Equus*, asses and zebras differ from the horse in numerous aspects of their physical character. The chestnuts (the horny callosities on the inside of the fore and hind legs) for instance, only occur on the front legs of asses and zebras, not on all four. There are five rather than six lumbar vertebrae; disproportionately long ears; an upright mane stopping short of a forelock and a tufted tail resembling that of the bovine. The back is straight and lower at the wither than the croup, whilst the feet are for the most part narrow, straight-sided and small.

The period of gestation in the horse is 11 months whereas that of the ass is 12. Then, of course, there is the characteristic bray rather than the neigh and whinny of the horse. Probably the most notable feature of the hemionid, although not of the domestic ass, or donkey, is the great length of the lower limbs which, when combined with the high croup conformation, allows the animal to move at surprisingly high speeds. (The same conformation characterises the cheetah and, of course, the greyhound.)

The Mongolian Kulan (*Equus hemionus hemionus*) for example, is capable of speeds of 35-40 mph and is more than capable of outrunning the desert wolf which, other than man, is its natural predator. R C Andrews, who studied the Kulan in the Gobi Desert between 1922 and 1925, recorded the case of a stallion, pursued by a car on the open steppe, which averaged 30mph over a distance of 16 miles.

The Kulan, called *jigetai* (long-eared) by the steppe people, who have reduced its numbers so significantly by hunting, stands between 12 and 13h.h (122-132cm). Unlike the members of the Asinus group (the donkeys) it does not have the dark stripe across the shoulder and bears a closer resemblance to the horse in respect of the feet and the voice, whilst the ears, too, are smaller than in other hemionids. Notably, it has nostrils much larger than either horse or domestic ass — an adaptation made necessary by the rarefied atmosphere. The coat colour varies according to the season. It is grey-white to accord with the winter snows and changes to a sandy red in summer.

The sub-species Kiang (*Equus hemionus kiang*) is the sole member of the Equidae inhabiting the Tibetan plateau, north of the mountain kingdoms of Bhutan, Sikkim and Nepal, on the very roof of the world, where the terrain never falls below 13,000ft above sea-level. In fact, the Kiang-steppe, immediately below the harsh, windswept desert habitat of the wild yak, extends up to 15,750ft and has a vegetation season lasting no longer than two or three months. The Kiang which is equipped with especially hard, thick lips, feeds in August and September on shrub growth and on the tough, sharp, but nutritious swamp grasses which would be an impossible diet for animals with more sensitive mouths. The grass, rich in silicic acid, causes the Kiangs to build up reserves of body fat against the harsh winter months during which food is sparse and lacking in nutrient content.

The Kiang herds, which live largely undisturbed on their rock-strewn plateau, are excessively shy and difficult to approach, quickly taking up wheeling defensive formations if they feel threatened. They are, however, more fortunate than the Kulan, for they are seen as sacred animals by the Tibetans and to hunt them would be quite inconceivable. That, however, would be no consideration with the Chinese who now occupy Tibet, although the habitat itself may be sufficiently inhospitable to deter any more serious depletion of the Kiang herds.

Just as the Asian Wild Horse was to be discovered by Col. Przewalskii, so the Kiang was first brought to the notice of the scientific world by another adventurer in the Great Game of Imperialist manoeuvring in Central Asia. This time it was an Englishman, William Moorcroft, ostensibly a veterinary surgeon in the employ of the Bengal Army, who is acknowledged as the father of Himalayan exploration. Often travelling in disguise he was among the earliest explorers of Ladakh and Kashmir and the first Englishman to set foot on the banks of the Oxus on his epic journey to Bokhara. Moorcroft died, it is said, of fever, in August 1825, when he was in his 60th year and is buried in an unmarked grave by that historic river.

Closely related to the Kulan and Kiang is the Indian onager or Ghorkhar (*Equus hemionus khur*). The Hindi word *ghork-har*, or more correctly *ghoor-khur* can be translated as 'wild mule'.

The now rare Indian Ghorkhar (Equus hemionus khur)
can still be found in small numbers in India's Rann of Kutch and some
may still survive in isolated areas of Baluchistan.

GRÉVY ZEBRA

The biggest of the zebra family is Grévy's zebra, classified in the sub-genus Dolichohippus. It is found in the desert country of Ethiopia, Somalia, and Kenya and is considered to be more closely related to the primitive equids than the other zebra species.

A hundred or more years ago the Ghorkhar could be found in the Rann of Kutch, in Gujerat, in Bikaner and adjoining states. It occurred also in the Sindh desert to the north and in Baluchistan west of the Indus. In all these desert-type areas it was shot extensively.

Nonetheless, as recently as 1956 it was estimated that the Ghorkhar herds, often as large as 200 animals, numbered 3-5,000. Within five years or so the population had been drastically reduced, probably by disease, and in 1969, after the Indian-Pakistan war, the Indian conservationist, E P Gee, considered that the Ghorkhar population did not exceed more than the 400 or so specimens confined to the Rann of Kutch. Today, numbers are probably even lower, but pockets may still survive in isolated areas of Baluchistan.

The habitat of the zebra is in southern Africa which once teemed with huge herds. Now only three species survive. The biggest of them at around 13.2h.h (138cm) is the handsome Grévy's Zebra, the most specialised of the zebra family which differs in proportion, coat colouring etc. from the others, and is more closely related to the primitive equids of perhaps 3.5 million years ago.

It inhabits low desert country in Kenya, Ethiopia and Somalia. The species, classified in the sub-genus *Dolichohippus* was named in 1882 after Jules Grévy, then President of France, was presented with a live specimen by King Menelik of Shoa (central Ethiopia).

The plump little animal found all over east and south-east Africa, and most frequently seen in captivity, is Burchell's Zebra belonging to the sub-genus *Hippotigris* (i.e. tiger-horse)

The third survivor of the once hugely varied zebra family is the Cape Mountain Zebra, still to be found, although in far smaller numbers than previously, to the north of the Orange river. It is the smallest of the zebras, about 12h.h (120cm) and the least numerous.

*Mountain Zebra of Cape Province, South Africa. It is
the smallest and the least numerous species of the zebra family.
Although there are obvious differences between horses and the asses
and zebras, all belong to the single genus Equus.*

Burchell's Zebra, belonging to the sub-genus
Hippotigris (i.e. tiger-horse), is the plump little animal found
all over east and south-east Africa and is the most numerous
of the surviving species.

THE NATURE OF THE HORSE

Wild Horse Refuges established throughout the western states have preserved the Mustang population. The first of them was created in Nevada in 1962.

All horses, whether in the wild or living in the domestic state, are herd animals whose character and instincts were formed largely as a result of environmental pressures exerted long before the domestication of the species by Man.

So long as the low jungle-type vegetation of the pre-Pleistocene period was a predominant feature of the prehistoric landscape, the early horse ancestors were browsing animals subsisting on shrub growth, which also gave them a measure of concealment that provided a defence against predators.

When jungle and swamplands gave way to treeless plains and savannah supporting wiry grasses, it was inevitable that the species would be compelled to adapt to the new circumstances if it was to survive.

The process by which a browsing animal, depending largely upon a defence system based on camouflage, evolved into a creature able to graze the hard savannah grasses and to ensure its survival by a defence mechanism based on detection and flight, took place over a period of millions of years.

By the Pleistocene period, some six million years ago, the prototype for *Equus*, the single-hooved *Pliohippus*, had become established as the only creditable precursor for the equine species, although there is little doubt that groups of less advanced animals, living possibly in the half-way house between the earlier jungle environment and the later plain lands, would have existed at the same time. About five million years later, *Pliohippus* had given way to *Equus*, an animal now fully equipped to meet the requirements of its environment physically and otherwise.

PHYSICAL ADAPTATION

To graze the wiry, abrasive grasses, stronger, higher crowned teeth developed which were protected by enamel and were heavily filled with cement so as to withstand the grinding action required of the molar teeth. The head and jaws altered in shape and the eyes were positioned more to the side of the head to give virtually an all-round vision even when grazing. The neck, too, became longer, so that the animal could feed easily at ground level, and when the head was raised it contributed significantly to the possible range of forward vision. Speed, of course, was increased by the development of longer legs and the swifter ligament-sprung action. The ears, too, acquired a greater length and mobility as the hearing became more acute. Indeed, the structure of the head acts virtually as a sound-box and is able to pick up sounds from a considerable distance very well. There are, in fact,

13 pairs of muscles involved in the movement of each ear and the ears can be directed individually to pick up sound through virtually 360°. Given, additionally, a strongly developed sense of smell, the horse was equipped to detect potential danger and then to use its speed to escape if it came under attack.

HEIGHTENED SENSES

To complete the defence mechanism a heightened awareness, or sensitivity, evolved in parallel with the physical development, and it remains a natural characteristic of the essentially highly strung horses of today. Possibly, the higher protein diet afforded by the grasses of the savannah contributed to the sharpening of the senses just as the feeding of grain or concentrates accentuate the nervous nature of the fit, modern competition horse kept in domestication.

BEHAVIOUR AND COMMUNICATION

Further protection and security was, and is, provided by the all-important herd environment, or by membership of a group within the herd.

Although there is now more or less general agreement on the necessity to preserve the Mustang, differences exist between bodies committed to conservation and the extremists opposing any form of control.

98

MUSTANG MARES AND FOAL, MONTANA

Of the wild horses, of whatever type or origin,

the archetypal Westener Will James wrote that, '... they really belong,

not to man, but to that country of junipers and sage, of deep

arroyas, mesas – and freedom.'

In the wild, the herd influence assumes great importance and the defence mechanism and overall awareness of feral animals is probably more developed than that of the domestic horse, although even in the latter the instincts acquired in the evolutionary process are never far from the surface.

It would be an over-simplification to suggest the complete subservience of a herd to a single, dominant stallion. In practice, wild herds, as well as those kept in the domestic state, divide into groups in which an order of precedence is quickly established. Obviously, the influence of the stallions is predominant, especially in the mating season, but that of the older mares is not insignificant. They are usually the group leaders and well able to control the boisterous behaviour of young colts. In the large semi-feral herds to be found in the eastern states of the old USSR, or in the Argentine, for instance, the herd leader is, more often than not, an old, experienced matriarch with a bell fastened round her neck (the 'bell mare'). The tinkle of the bell acts as a guide for both the herd and the herdsmen.

Whilst stallions are nearly always dominant in character it would be wrong to regard mares as always being submissive. Many mares, can be very dominant and forceful. Conversely, whilst geldings in the domestic state may retain dominant features, many will be submissive in nature.

The prime motivation of horse herds in the wild is the continual search for food, the herd moving slowly, so long as it is not disturbed, from one grazing ground to the next. Whilst young horses, like the young of all species, indulge in play, 'horse-play', in fact, and will gallop about to let off steam, the herd only gallops when alarmed by what is perceived to be a threat to its safety, whatever form that may take.

At certain times of the year the need to reproduce becomes paramount and sexually orientated behaviour is more in evidence. Although horses are not territorial animals, stallions emphasise their presence and their dominant influence over a group of mares by scent-marking the area containing the harem. They do this by dropping piles of faeces and by urination, frequently urinating over the faeces or urine made by the mares within the group.

The language of communication between horses is complex and very sophisticated. There is an obvious body-language but there is also communication through the senses, which are far more developed than in the human. Smell plays an important part in the social structure of a herd with smell messages, pheromones, being constantly produced by the skin glands. In this way a foal instinctively recognises its dam and vice-versa. Similarly, groups exude a corporate odour, easily recognisable to those animals belonging to them, whilst a mare in oestrus emits pheremones that indicate clearly to the stallion that she is ready to mate. The scent message is further reinforced by physical signals. She will 'flash' the vulva, for instance, and will hold the tail to one side in the mating posture which facilitates the stallion's entry. Should she not be ready to accept the stallion she makes her feelings known just as unmistakably, indicating her unwillingness by baring the teeth, laying back the ears and by biting and kicking the too-ardent suitor.

A stallion will check continually the oestrus cycle by smelling the mare's vulva and her urine and as she comes close to oestrus he will engage in tactile stimulation, licking her sexual organ and indulging in flehmen, the curious curling back of the lip which is an almost certain accompaniment of sexual excitement, although flehmen can also be provoked in both males and females in response to strong and unusual smells. (The conception rates in wild or semi-feral stock is much higher than that experienced at domestic studs practising in-hand mating, largely because the in-hand method limits the natural courtship.)

Tactile signals are employed in mutual grooming and are of particular importance in the relationship between mare and foal. Vocal communication is more limited. Squeals and grunts accompany aggression and/or excitement, whilst the snort given with raised head and pricked ears can be an indication of something that has attracted the attention and may constitute a potential danger. The snort also acts to clear the respiratory passages in anticipation of sudden flight involving violent exertion. Mares whicker reassuringly to their foals and a horse may whinny if separated from its group or if it is unusually excited.

The ears are also used as a means of communication. Pricked forward they express their owner's strong interest in some object and at the same time the message is clarified still more by an unmistakable posture of tension. Relaxation is made apparent by an opposite posture, a rested foot, a lowering of the head and flaccid ears. Anger, aggression and irritation are expressed by the ears being laid back on the head, and is supported by teeth being bared and the animal showing the white of the eyes.

Whilst differences will obviously occur within the herd structure, fights between stallions that result in death or serious injury are very rare. But then horses, unlike carnivores, are not aggressive animals by nature.

Colorado supports significant wild horse herds, the control
of which, as in other Western states, is the responsibility of the
Bureau of Land Management.

Mustang stock is naturally hardy, and just as naturally,

wild and wary of humans. Properly handled, broken and trained

they can become reliable mounts but they cannot be kept as pets

by the well-intentioned but inexperienced.

Ecologists and wildlife biologists are united on the need
to control the horse population so as to maintain proper balance
between the habitat and the other animals involved.

The Mustang, for most Americans, is seen as
part of the Western tradition and heritage, embodying the
historic and pioneering spirit of the West.

'Our only concern is for the welfare of wild horses
and burros, other wildlife, and preservation of the public land resource
without which man himself, along with all other creature dependent upon
it, cannot survive' (Velma Johnston).

GLOSSARY

Appaloosa

Spotted coat pattern in a variety of forms. The Appaloosa is a recognised world breed.

Barb

Ancient North African breed held to be the principal influence in the Spanish or Iberian horses.

Breed

Equine group which for reasons of habitat or kinship share characteristics of height, colour, conformation, etc. In domestic terms a group bred selectively over a sufficient period to ensure the consistent production of stock that has in common clearly, defined, characteristics of height colour, conformation, action etc. and the pedigrees of which are, additionally, registered in a stud book maintained by the breed society.

Croup

The point of the croup is the highest part of the quarters and slopes towards the root of the tail (or dock).

Dorsal Stripe

A continuous stripe of dark hair extending from the neck to the tail. Usually found in dun horses and always in asses and donkeys.

Dun

Basic colour pattern is yellow or tan but a bluish colour ranging through slate to grey mouse is also found. Dun patterns are usually accompanied by a dorsal stripe, black mane and tail and either black lower limbs or black bars round the lower legs (zebra bars). American terms in general use are Buckskin (yellow/tan); Grulla (mouse or blue) and a red dun is also recognised.

Eel Stripe

See Dorsal Stripe

Equus caballus

The name given to modern Equidae. The 'true' horse developed from a progression which can be traced from the Eocene period of 60 million years ago. It evolved in recognisable form about 1m years ago. (The Latin *fons caballinus* was applied to the fountain Hippocrene, said to have been made by a stroke of the foot of the winged Pegasus; hence 'fountains of inspiration'.)

Equus przewalskii przewalskii poliakov

The Asiatic Wild Horse of Mongolia, the discovery of which in 1879 is attributed to Col. N M Przewalskii. It is regarded as the foundation, along with the Tarpan and Forest Horse, for the modern horse breeds and types.

Gestation

The gestation period of a horse extends over 11 months and of an ass over 12 months.

Heavy Horse

One belonging to any of the heavy, draught breeds i.e. Shire, Clydesdale, Belgian etc.

Height

Traditionally the height of Equidae is expressed in hands, a medieval unit of measurement based on the width of a man's hand. It equals 4in (10.16cm) and is expressed as h.h. i.e. hands high. Thus 14.2h.h. refers to an animal standing at fourteen and a half hands or 14h.h and 2in. The measurement is taken from the highest point of the withers to the ground. Increasingly, however height is being expressed in centimetres, a trend that is likely to continue.

Horse and Pony

There is a division between the horse and the pony, the latter being applied to animals below 15h.h (152cm). In fact, the difference is not of height but of proportion. In the horse the distance from wither to ground exceeds the length of the body largely on account of the length of the leg. The opposite is true of the pony.

Ice-Tail

Thick fan-like growth at the top of the tail providing protection against snow, rain etc.

In-breeding

Mating between sire/daughter, dam (mother)/son, etc. Literally incest breeding. It can be used as a selective breeding tool to enhance certain characteristics, but within small, feral groups the practice frequently results in degeneration of the stock.

Light Horse

A horse intended for riding and carriage work as opposed to the heavy, agricultural draught horse or a pony.

Line-Breeding

Selective mating of animals with a common ancestor some generations removed so as to accentuate and perpetuate a particular feature.

Longevity

Very variable, but on average 25 years.

Mules and Hinnies

A mule is a cross between a jackass (a male donkey) and a mare. A hinny is a cross between a horse and a donkey mare.

Norfolk Rooster (Trotter)

A powerful trotting roadster (either under saddle or in harness) developed in England during the seventeenth and eighteenth centuries from the same source of Eastern blood as the Thoroughbred and from which the Hackney derives. The roadster no longer exists as a breed but its influence is present in most European breeds and it is at the root of the American Standardbred.

Paces

There are four natural equine paces or gaits – walk, trot, canter and gallop – as well as a number of specialised ones based largely on the pacing or ambling gaits.

Pacer

A horse employing a lateral action at trot rather than moving the legs in diagonal pairs ie. the pacer uses the near fore and hind together, followed by the off fore and hind. Many harness racers, notably the American Standardbred use the pacing gait.

Palomino

A gold colour accompanied by a silvery white mane and tail.

Pinto or Paint

American term for part coloured horses. In the USA these horses are represented by two 'breed' societies. Pinto coat patterns are divided into two types: tobiano and overo. The former is a white coat marked with patches of solid colour, the latter is a coloured coat marked with splashes of white.

Skewbald

A term referring to a part-coloured coat which has large white patches on a different body colour.

Stud

A breeding establishment, a stud farm, also 'stud' as referring to stallion.

Thoroughbred

The Thoroughbred racehorse evolved in England during the seventeenth and eighteenth centuries on the basis of imported Eastern stock. The word Thoroughbred, indicating a pure breed, first appeared in 1821 in Vol II of the *English General Stud Book* (GSB). The genealogical records of all British and Irish Thoroughbreds are recorded in the GSB.

Toad-Eye

A 'hooded' eye giving additional protection against the weather.

Type

Horses of mixed breeding and of no fixed character which do not qualify for entry in a stud book, ie. hunter, cob, hack.

Teeth

At six years the horse has a 'full mouth' of permanent teeth. Each jaw has twelve molar teeth and six incisor teeth. Male horses have an additional tooth, 'tush', situated behind the incisor teeth.

Wither

The wither is the highest part of the back between the shoulder blades.

Zebra Marking

Bands of dark hair round the lower limbs. It is found in duns and asses.

BIBLIOGRAPHY

The Horses of Sable Island, Barbara J Christie (Pentheric Press Ltd 1980)

The Foals of Epona, Anthony Dent and Daphne Machin-Goodall (Gallery Press 1962)

The Ultimate Horse Book, E Hartley Edwards (Dorling Kindersley 1991)

Horses, Asses and Zebras, Colin P Groves (David and Charles 1994)

The Exmoor Pony, J G and M G Speed (Countrywide Livestock Ltd 1976)

The Wild Horse Controversy, Heather Smith Thomas (A S Barnes and Co. 1979)

The Empire of Equus, David P Willoughby (A S Barnes and Co. 1974)